To cindy

who has tau[ght me so]

much . . .

Lucy

December 10 1974

OPPOSITES

OPPOSITES

written and illustrated by
RICHARD WILBUR

New York
HARCOURT BRACE JOVANOVICH, INC.

ISBN 0-15-258720-9

*Library of Congress Catalog Card Number: 72-88175
Printed in the United States of America*

First edition

B   C   D   E   F   G   H   I   J

For Aaron

OPPOSITES

1

What is the opposite of *nuts*?
It's *soup*! Let's have no ifs or buts.
In any suitable repast
The soup comes first, the nuts come last.
Or that is what *sane* folk advise;
You're nuts if you think otherwise.

2

What is the opposite of *flying*?
For birds, it would be *just not trying*.

Perhaps the opposite for us
Would be *to take a train or bus*.

3

The opposite of *foot* is what?
A *mountain top*'s one answer, but
If you are thinking of a bed,
The opposite of foot is *head*.
To ancient generals, of course,
The opposite of foot was *horse*.

4

What is the opposite of *cheese*?
For mice, it's *anything you please*.
So fond are they of cheese, that mice
Think nothing else is very nice.

I too like cheese, I must admit.
I'm certainly not opposed to it.

5

The opposite of *junk* is *stuff*
Which someone thinks is good enough,

Or *any vessel on the seas*
That isn't in the least Chinese.

6

What is the opposite of *string*?
It's *gnirts*, which doesn't mean a thing.

7

The opposite of *standing still*
Is *walking up or down a hill,*
Running backwards, creeping, crawling,
Leaping off a cliff and falling,

Turning somersaults in gravel,
Or any other mode of travel.

8

What is the opposite of *riot*?
It's *lots of people keeping quiet*.

9

The opposite of a *hole*'s a *heap*
Just as high as the hole is deep.
How deep's the hole? Go on and measure,
If it will give you any pleasure.

10

What is the opposite of *fox*?
Foxes are clever, while the *ox*,
So we are told, could not be duller:
But is it opposite in color?

The fox is reddish-brown in hue;
Perhaps *a greenish ox* would do.

11

The opposite of *making faces*
Is *not indulging in grimaces*,
Wrinkling your nose, with tongue stuck out,
And rolling both your eyes about,
But letting eyes, and mouth, and nose
Remain entirely in repose.
It's true, however, that a *very*
Fixed expression can be scary.

12

What is the opposite of *two*?
A lonely me, a lonely you.

13

What is the opposite of *doe*?
The answer's *buck*, as you should know.
A buck *is* dough, you say? Well, well,
Clearly you don't know how to spell.
Moreover, get this through your head:
The current slang for dough is *bread*.

14

What is the opposite of *penny*?
I'm sorry, but there isn't any—
Unless you count the change, I guess,
Of someone who is *penniless*.

When people flip a penny, its
Two *sides*, of course, are opposites.

I'll flip one now. Go on and choose:
Which is it, heads or tails? You lose.

15

The opposite of *squash*? Offhand,
I'd say that it might be *expand*,
Enlarge, *uncrumple*, or *inflate*.

However, on a dinner plate
With yellow vegetables and green,
The opposite of squash is *bean*.

16

What is the opposite of *actor*?
The answer's very simple: *tractor*.
I said that just because it rhymes,
As lazy poets do at times.

However, to be more exact,
An actor's one who likes to act
King Lear in some unlikely plot,
Pretending to be what he's not.

The opposite of *actor*, friend,
Is *someone who does not pretend*,
But is *himself*, like you and me.
I'm Romeo. Who might you be?

17

There's more than one way to be right
About the opposite of *white*,
And those who merely answer *black*
Are very, very single-track.
They make one want to scream, "I beg
Your pardon, but within an egg
(A fact known to the simplest folk)
The opposite of white is *yolk*!"

18

The opposite of *doughnut*? Wait
A minute while I meditate.

This isn't easy. Ah, I've found it!
A cookie with a hole around it.

19

Because what's *present* doesn't last,
The opposite of it is *past*.
Or if you choose to look ahead,
Future's the opposite instead.
Or look around to see what's here,
And *absent* things will not appear.
There's one more opposite of *present*
That's really almost too unpleasant:
It is *when someone takes away*
Something with which you like to play.

20

What is the opposite of *hat*?
It isn't hard to answer that.
It's *shoes*, for shoes and hat together
Protect our two extremes from weather.

Between these two extremes there lies
A middle, which you would be wise
To clothe as well, or you'll be chilly
And run the risk of looking silly.

21

The opposites of *earth* are two,
And which to choose is up to you.
One opposite is called *the sky*,
And that's where larks and swallows fly;
But angels, there, are few if any,
Whereas in *heaven* there are many.
Well, which word are you voting for?
Do birds or angels please you more?
It's very plain that you are loath
To choose. All right, we'll keep them both.

22

The opposite of a *cloud* could be
A white reflection in the sea,

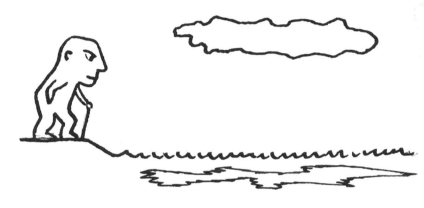

Or *a huge blueness in the air,*
Caused by a cloud's not being there.

23

Not to have any *hair* is called
Hairlessness, or being *bald*.
It is a fine thing to be hairy,
Yet it's not always necessary.
Bald heads on men are very fine,
Particularly if they shine,
And who conceivably could wish
To see a hairy frog or fish?

Some creatures, though, do well to wear
Λ normal covering of hair.
I don't think I should care to know
Those hairless dogs of Mexico
Who ramble naked out of doors
And must be patted on their pores.

24

What is the opposite of *Cupid*?
If you don't know, you're pretty stupid.
It's someone with a crossbow who
Delights in shooting darts at you,
Not with the kind intention of
Persuading you to fall in love,
But to be mean, and make you shout,
"I hate you," "Ouch," and "Cut it out."

25

What is the opposite of a *shoe*?
Either the *right* or *left* will do,
Depending on which one you've got.
The question's foolish, is it not?

26

What is the opposite of *fleet*?
Someone who's *slow* and drags his feet.

Another's an *armada* that'll
Engage the first fleet in a battle.

27

What is the opposite of *July*?
That's hard to answer, but I'll try.
In San Francisco and Quebec,
Duluth, Big Forks, Mamaroneck,
And every other city here
In the upper Western Hemisphere,
July can be extremely hot;
But far to southward it is not.
The month can be extremely chill
In Paraguay or in Brazil,
And furthermore, July can mean a
Blizzard or so in Argentina.
These unexpected facts are why
The opposite of July's *July*.

28

What is the opposite of *bat*?
It's easy enough to answer that.
A bat sleeps upside down in trees,
Whereas a *horse*, with equal ease,
Can sleep while upright in his stall.

Another answer might be *ball*.

29

The opposite of *well* is *sick*.

Another answer's *to be quick*
And tell what you have got to tell,
Without a lot of "Well . . . well . . . well . . ."

30

The opposite of *tiller*? Well,
It's *when some farmer in the dell*
Has grown so lazy that by now
He lacks the energy to plow.

A *bowsprit* also comes to mind,
Since, like a tiller, it's a kind
Of stick, and since on sailing craft
The bowsprit's fore, the tiller aft.

I also think of *butter*, *brads*,
Shoe polish, *cannon*, *shoulder pads*,
Daisies, and *stock exchange*, and *goat*,
Since none of these can steer a boat.

31

The opposite of *fast* is *loose*,
And if you doubt it you're a goose.
"Nonsense!" you cry. "As you should know,
The opposite of fast is *slow*."
Well, let's not quarrel: have a chair
And see what's on the bill of fare.

We should agree on this at least:
The opposite of fast is *feast*.

What is the opposite of a *prince*?
A *frog* must be the answer, since,
As all good fairy stories tell,
When some witch says a magic spell,
Causing the prince to be disguised
So that he won't be recognized,
He always ends up green and sad
And sitting on a lily pad.

33

The opposite of a *king*, I'm sure,
Is someone humble and obscure—
A *peasant*, or some *wretched soul*
Who begs through life with staff and bowl.

Another opposite's the *queen*,
If she is quarrelsome and mean.

34

The opposite of *spit*, I'd say,
Would be *a narrow cove or bay*.

(There is another sense of *spit*,
But I refuse to think of it.
It stands opposed to *all refined
And decent instincts of mankind*!)

35

What is the opposite of *ball*?
It's *meteor*. Though meteors fall
As balls do, and like balls are round,
And though they sometimes hit the ground,
They don't know how to bounce or roll
And merely make a dreadful hole.

36

The opposite of *trunk* could be
The taproot of a cedar tree.
In terms of elephants, however,
The answer *tail* is rather clever.

Another answer is *when all*
Your things are tied up in a ball
And carried on your head, for lack
Of anything in which to pack.

37

The opposite of *post*, were you
On horseback, would be *black and blue*;

Another answer is *to fail*
To put your letters in the mail.

38

What is the opposite of *mirror*?
The answer hardly could be clearer:
It's *anything which, on inspection,*
Is not all full of your reflection.

For instance, it would be no use
To brush your hair before a moose,
Or try a raincoat on for size
While looking at a swarm of flies.

39

The opposite of *opposite*?
That's much too difficult. I quit.